OFF WE GO!
TO JAIPUR, TO JAIPUR

TALKING CUB
Speaking Tiger Books LLP
4381/4 Ansari Road, Daryaganj, New Delhi – 110002, India

Published in Talking Cub, an imprint of Speaking Tiger Books, in association with INTACH in hardback in 2021

Text and illustrations copyright © INTACH 2021

ISBN: 978-93-90477-82-1
eISBN: 978-93-90477-73-9

10 9 8 7 6 5 4 3 2 1

Designed by Aniruddha Mukherjee for Syllables27, a specialised children's content outfit run by the authors to produce books for children on a turn-key basis for various publishers and organisations.

All rights reserved.
No part of this publication may be reproduced, transmitted, or stored in a retrieval system, in any form or by any means, electronic, mechanical, photocopying, recording or otherwise, without the prior permission of the publisher.

This book is sold subject to the condition that it shall not, by way of trade or otherwise, be lent, resold, hired out, or otherwise circulated, without the publisher's prior consent, in any form of binding or cover other than that in which it is published.

OFF WE GO!
TO JAIPUR, TO JAIPUR

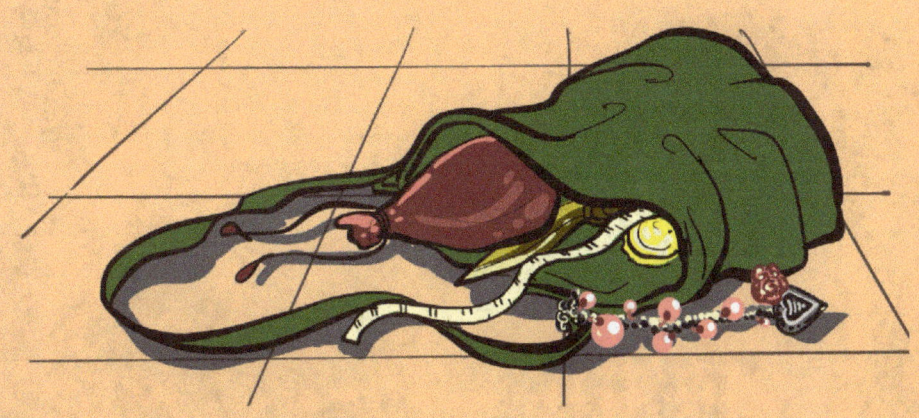

WRITTEN BY ARTHY MUTHANNA SINGH AND MAMTA NAINY
ILLUSTRATED BY PRIYANKAR GUPTA

'5 across. The residence of a ruler. 6 letters. Ends in...' Pia blinked at the newspaper through her big, round glasses.

'The word is "palace". Ends in "e",' Kavya crowed, as she bit into the pyaaz kachori she was having in the restaurant of the Raj Niwas Hotel. 'How about a different word, Pia?' Kavya added, stifling a giggle. 'Nine letters. Clue: Flickers sometimes but doesn't go on until much later. Could it be T-u-b-e L-i-g-h-t?'

'Kavyaaaa,' Mamma glared at her. 'Your sister is five years younger than you. If she takes more time than you to think things over, so what?'

'What's that?' Kavya said hurriedly, in her bid to distract her mother. She pointed to a piece of news on the back page of the newspaper that carried the crossword Pia was solving.

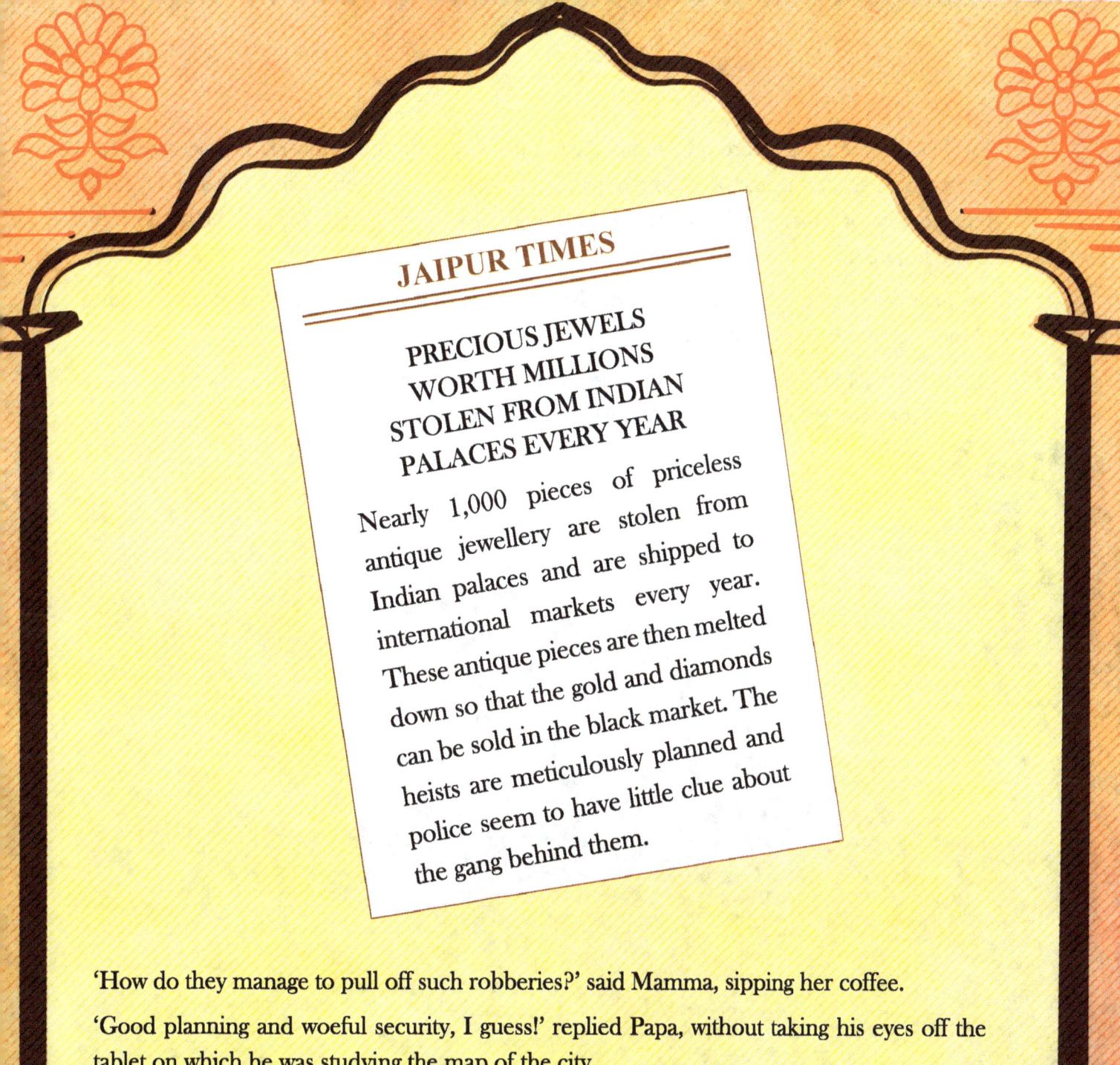

JAIPUR TIMES

PRECIOUS JEWELS WORTH MILLIONS STOLEN FROM INDIAN PALACES EVERY YEAR

Nearly 1,000 pieces of priceless antique jewellery are stolen from Indian palaces and are shipped to international markets every year. These antique pieces are then melted down so that the gold and diamonds can be sold in the black market. The heists are meticulously planned and police seem to have little clue about the gang behind them.

'How do they manage to pull off such robberies?' said Mamma, sipping her coffee.

'Good planning and woeful security, I guess!' replied Papa, without taking his eyes off the tablet on which he was studying the map of the city.

'At least something interesting happens in this city with no snow-clad mountains or far-reaching sea,' said Kavya, rolling her eyes. 'It would have been so much better had we gone to Goa or Mussoorie!' she ranted for the nth time since they'd boarded the train from Delhi to Jaipur.

'Jaipur may not have the mountains or the sea, Didi, but it has palaces! And palaces are always full of mystery!' said Pia.

'Let's see what kind of mystery awaits us,' Kavya tut-tutted as she gobbled up the last bit of her kachori and gulped down the last dregs of her buttermilk.

The taxi arrived soon after and Pia, Kavya, Mamma and Papa were off to the first stop in the oh-so-long 'List of Places to Visit in Jaipur' that Papa had drawn.

Through the window of the taxi, Pia saw men with the most colourful turbans and women in long skirts and flowing dupattas. The taxi drove past beautiful buildings that looked very old. 'But why are all the buildings pink?' Pia wondered aloud.

'Because it's the "Pink City", duh!' Kavya remarked.

'That's right!' said the taxi driver with a smile. 'But do you know why the city was painted pink? To welcome an important guest! In 1876, Prince Albert Edward, the eldest son of Queen Victoria, visited the Maharaja of Jaipur. To welcome the Prince, the Maharaja ordered the city of Jaipur to be repainted in terracotta pink – a colour that traditionally signifies hospitality. This move earned the city its name "Pink City".'

'Interesting!' said Papa.

The taxi came to a halt in front of a huge gate with rich decorations.

'Here we are. At the City Palace,' announced the taxi driver. 'The Maharaja of Jaipur, Sawai Jai Singh II, divided the city into nine blocks and this royal palace, where the royal family still lives, is right at the centre of the city. There are three main entry gates to the Palace. This is the Udai Pol or the stable gate. The other entrance is the Virendra Pol. And the third entrance, the Tripolia gate, is reserved for the entry of the royal family into the palace.'

As the family got down from the taxi, a small, bald man came running towards them. 'Khamma Ghani!' the man said with his hand placed on his chest and his head bent low. 'Guide, Sir, Guide?' he asked.

'I think we'd need a guide,' said Papa. 'How much?'

'Five hundred, sir. All the history in just 500. Not a bad deal, Sir!'

'Okay,' said Papa.

The guide took them through the gate, across the courtyard towards a splendid structure. 'Padharo sa,' he said as he led them inside.

They entered a large room with high ceilings and pale green chandeliers. The floor was paved with intricate mosaic tiles. On the walls were large wall paintings and photographs. There was no furniture except for two thrones at the centre, with big velvet bolsters to rest on, and lots of chairs around them.

'This is the Sabha Niwas or Diwan-e-Aam,' said the guide. 'The Hall of Audience, where the Maharaja held his durbar.'

A little distance away was an open square hall. This hall too was decorated with plush chandeliers and delicate wall art.

'This is Sarvato Bhadra or Diwan-e-Khaas,' said the guide. 'This is the hall that the Maharaja of Jaipur used for intimate gatherings.'

INSIDE THE CITY PALACE...

Apart from the Diwan-e-Aam and Diwan-e-Khaas, there are many other pavilions to check out inside the City Palace.

Mubarak Palace or the welcome palace. You will find a fine selection of textiles here.

Chandra Mahal or the moon palace. It stands tall in the inner courtyard of the City Palace.

Sileh Khana, the arms and armoury museum. It can fill you up with more chills than ever, with swords used in wars, scissor-action daggers and many other weapons!

Just then, Pia saw two huge sparkling vessels kept in the middle of the open hall.

'Look, Didi,' she said excitedly. 'Such big vessels!'

'Yes, they're huge,' said Kavya. 'But what are these for?'

'These are the world's largest silver vessels,' said the guide. 'Each of these weighs about 340 kilograms and has a capacity of 4000 litres. They were made from 14,000 melted silver coins. These vessels were specially commissioned by Maharaja Sawai Madho Singh II to carry the water of the Ganges to drink when he went to England in 1901. These vessels are named as Gangajalis.'

'So much water for just one trip?' asked Pia.

'No wonder the world is facing a severe water crisis,' joked Kavya.

The guide took them to the textile gallery next. It had glass-walled rooms with textiles and carpets on display. There was also a special exhibition going on of the Maharaja's jewellery – necklaces and bracelets, brooches and belts, rings and watch chains, buttons and cufflinks and even turban ornaments. But there was this one golden brooch with little birds studded with jewels that Pia couldn't get her eyes off.

'Look at this, Didi! It's soooo beautiful,' Pia said, pointing to the golden brooch.

'It's the Maharaja's famous golden brooch,' said the guide. 'It's the one he wore for his wedding. The jewels on the brooch throw off flashes of different colours when tilted!'

'Like a ka...ka...la... what's that word, Didi?'

'Kaleidoscope,' said Kavya.

'Yes, kaleidoscope,' repeated Pia.

Suddenly an alarm rang in one of the other galleries.

'What's this alarm?' Mamma asked.

'Let's go and check,' said the guide.

Everyone rushed to the other gallery. It turned out that someone had tried to draw a moustache on one of Maharani Sahiba's famous portraits. The culprit, of course, was fined.

'When will people learn to take care of our heritage and not destroy it like this?' said the guide irritably as they came out of the gallery.

PALACES OF JAIPUR

Apart from the City Palace, there are many other palaces in Jaipur such as Rambagh Palace, Rajmahal Palace, Samode Palace, Diggi Palace, Harimahal Palace and Jal Mahal Palace.

As they were walking back towards the gallery with the jewellery exhibit, Pia saw a beautiful photograph on a wall. It was of the Maharaja playing polo. Pia was walking towards it to have a closer look when suddenly she bumped into a fierce-looking man with a long moustache. He was wearing a colourful turban and holding a small bag which fell down from his hand, spilling its assorted contents – a measuring tape; a sharp, knife-like thing; and a velvet pouch with a small shiny object jutting out. Pia couldn't see the object clearly but it had a multi-coloured glint to it.

'Why don't you watch where you're going?' the man snapped.

Pia remembered seeing this man in the hall where the Maharaja's jewellery was on display. He had stared at the golden brooch for a long time.

'What is that?' asked Pia, pointing at the shiny object.

'None of your business,' the man shot back, quickly pushing back the slightly exposed bit of the object into the pouch. 'Just watch your steps before you do some real damage,' he said and quickly made an exit.

Pia found a crumpled piece of paper lying on the floor. It must have fallen out from the man's bag, she thought. She was about to run after him to return the piece of paper when she felt a tap on her shoulder.

Pia turned around. Kavya was standing behind her. 'Where are you going?' she asked.

'Umm...nowhere!' said Pia and stuffed the paper into her pocket.

Suddenly, they heard a commotion in the gallery of the jewellery exhibit.

They both rushed to the gallery. 'What happened?' Kavya asked Mamma.

'The Maharaja's brooch has been stolen!' replied Mamma.

'What?' Pia asked shockingly. 'We just saw it minutes ago!'

'Yes, someone seems to have pinched it in a minute's time!' said Papa.

The entire security force of the palace reached the gallery in panic. In less than a few minutes, policemen too swarmed the museum.

After a lot of frisking and questioning by the police, Mamma, Papa, Kavya and Pia finally came out of the palace.

'How could the brooch go missing in broad daylight with so many people around?' asked Mamma. 'First somebody tried to destroy a work of art and then this,' she continued.

'Maybe they're both linked,' said Kavya. 'Maybe the portrait of the Maharani was vandalised to distract security and the crowds. And when all of us rushed to the portrait gallery, someone stole the brooch!'

'Yes! That must be it,' exclaimed Pia. 'And the man I bumped into must have stolen the brooch. He was looking at it for a long time!'

'Which man?' asked Kavya.

'The one who was in a tearing hurry...the one who dropped this piece of paper,' replied Pia as she took out the crumpled paper from her pocket and unrolled it.

'Looks like a poem,' she said and read aloud what was written on the paper.

Begin the journey where the sun rays fall,
Take it to the White Bishop as the king stands tall.
Not far is a palace where blushing winds blow,
Blue God's crown has a jewel missing in the third row.
Ride to the beautiful hills of shadows and sound,
There you will find a fireball, big and very round.
Walk to the bazaar where trinkets are sold,
Look for the shop with painted riches quite old.
Neither too high, nor too low,
The jewels shall sparkle, all aglow.

'A badly written poem,' remarked Kavya.

'Yes, but what does it mean?' asked Pia, moving her index finger across the rows of words.

Mamma stared at Pia puzzled. 'Stop reading too much into this poem. It doesn't mean anything at all,' she said.

'Maybe it does,' Kavya insisted. 'Maybe it holds a secret that can help us solve the mystery of the Maharaja's missing brooch.'

Pia gave out an excited laugh. 'Yes! Mystery.'

'How?' asked Mamma. 'There are no clues in the poem.'

'Maybe there are,' said Kavya, putting on her best Sherlock Holmes manner. 'What if we try and solve the puzzle in the poem? What's the first line, Pia?'

'Here are the first two lines: *Begin the journey where the sunrays fall… Take it to the white bishop as the king stands tall.*' Pia raised the piece of paper close to her face and peered intently at the words.

There was a brief silence.

'Well,' Papa said after a pause, 'that sounds like a most unlikely clue. As far as I know, sunrays fall everywhere!'

'If the message in the poem was obvious to one and all, Papa, then the secret wouldn't be much of a secret!' said Kavya.

'This is no secret poem. And stop looking for non-existent mysteries everywhere, you two!' Papa said as he saw the guide running towards them.

'I have been looking for you inside, Sir!' said the guide, panting between words. 'This is the first time that something like this has happened in the palace – everyone is being checked, even regulars like us!'

'We still can't believe that somebody stole the brooch right in front of so many people,' Papa said. 'We haven't even seen the entire palace yet,' he added, after a brief pause.

'There's the famous Jantar Mantar just around the corner, Sir. Should I take you there?' the guide asked.

'Is it similar to the Jantar Mantar in Delhi?' asked Mamma.

'Yes, Madam. Both were built by Maharaja Jai Singh II, the founder of the city of Jaipur. In fact, he commissioned the Jantar Mantar observatories at multiple places in India, including this one in Jaipur which is the best preserved and the largest of all.'

'Are there huge clocks in this observatory to tell time?' asked Pia.

'Not really,' said the guide. 'The instruments in Jantar Mantar are angled in such a way that the sun's rays fall on the instruments and, by looking at the shadow cast by them, one can tell the time.'

'Begin the journey where the sunrays fall,' Kavya murmured thoughtfully.

'Begin the journey where the sunrays fall,' Pia repeated in a whisper and jumped up a foot or two.

'We definitely must go to the observatory,' Kavya and Pia chorused.

Kavya, Pia, Mamma and Papa followed the guide to a place that looked like a collection of some bizarre stone sculptures.

'The word Jantar Mantar comes from the Sanskrit words yantra mantr, meaning "instrument of calculation",' said the guide as they entered the observatory complex. 'These are the gadgets of the olden times!'

The family walked through the maze of the various yantras in the Jantar Mantar complex – each interpreting either planetary movements or time.

'What's that gigantic instrument?' Kavya asked suddenly, pointing at a huge triangular structure some distance away.

'Oh, that! That's the king of all instruments here – the Samrat Yantra. It is the biggest sundial in the world. It can tell time to the accuracy of two seconds,' the guide said. 'And it stands 27 metres tall.'

Just then, a man came to them. He was wearing a white dhoti-kurta and had an unusually long neck. 'Can you please take a picture of me against this yantra,' he requested the guide, outstretching his hand with the mobile phone.

'Of course!' said the guide and clicked his picture.

The man thanked the guide and was walking away when Pia noticed his bag. It looked exactly like the bag of the moustached man whom she had bumped into in the City Palace.

Pia tugged at her sister's shirt and whispered, 'Didi, this man is carrying the same bag that the man in the City Palace was carrying.'

'How can you be so sure, Pia?' Kavya whispered back.

'Look at the small beaded charm hanging from the bag. I remember it clearly!'

'Oh!' Kavya's voice quivered in excitement. '*Take it to the White Bishop where the king stands tall*...it matches! Maybe the White Bishop is this man in white with an unusually long, camel-like neck.'

'But where's the king, Didi?'

'The king of yantras, Pia. The Samrat Yantra!'

'This must be it, Didi!' Pia's eyes widened. 'He would have the Maharaja's brooch.'

But when Kavya and Pia looked around for the man in white, he was nowhere in sight.

Pia's face fell. 'We missed him, Didi,' she said.

'Don't worry, Pia,' said Kavya. 'We shall find him.'

As the family came out of the complex, Pia and Kavya kept an eye out for the man in white.

Papa took out his long list of places to visit from his pocket. 'Hawa Mahal is close by, right?' he asked the guide.

'Yes, Sir,' said the guide. 'Just five minutes away. Shall I take you there?' he asked.

Papa nodded.

The guide got them a tuk-tuk auto.

'What's Hawa Mahal?' asked Pia, bobbing up and down through the bumpy ride.

'It's the most iconic structure in Jaipur,' said Papa. 'The Palace of Winds.'

'Palace of Winds,' mumbled Pia. 'That sounds familiar.'

'Psst! The third line of the poem,' said Kavya. *'Not far is a palace where blushing winds blow...'*

'Oh, yes!' murmured Pia.

The tuk-tuk skated along the maze of narrow alleys with a lot of food carts on both sides, selling everything from paani ke bataashe to mirchi pakodas and samosas.

'Shouldn't we just stop by and have something, Didi?' Pia asked Kavya. 'I'm hungry.'

'Don't be a greedy hog, Pia,' Kavya told her. 'The food won't run away but the White Bishop will!'

The corners of Pia's mouth turned down. But she agreed with Kavya.

STREET FOOD OF JAIPUR

Whether it's dal baati choorma, kachoris or ghevar, Jaipur is a food-lover's paradise. The street food of Jaipur too is drool-worthy – you will find the yummiest chaat, samosas, rabri and more on the streets of Jaipur.

The tuk-tuk finally stopped in front of a huge pink structure which had many windows.

'This is the Hawa Mahal,' said the guide. 'The tallest building in the world with no foundation.'

'No foundation?' Mamma asked. 'What does it stand on then?'

'This five-storeyed building manages to stand upright without a foundation because of its curved shape,' the guide told her.

'How amazing!' exclaimed Pia. 'But who thought of this brilliant idea?' she asked.

'It was designed in 1799 by the master architect Lal Chand Ustad on Maharaja Sawai Pratap Singh's orders.'

'And why are there so many windows?' asked Kavya, as they climbed up the stairs and reached the first floor.

'In earlier times, the women of the royal families were not to be seen by the public. So the Maharaja built a palace with many windows so that they could look at the streets, markets, and festival celebrations without being seen,' answered the guide. 'Do you know how many windows there are in Hawa Mahal?' he asked and then without waiting for an answer, answered himself. 'Nine hundred and fifty-three!'

'The windows also allow winds to flow through them and keep the palace very cool. It made the ideal summer palace for the royalty,' the guide continued after a brief pause.

'A Palace of Winds, it is,' Kavya whispered into Pia's ear. 'But what about the fourth line in the poem which talks about a god, his crown and the third row?'

'Maybe there's some crown hidden somewhere here...' Pia whispered back.

Kavya and Pia started looking here and there. Staring at the windows, Pia said, 'This palace looks like a honeycomb with all its windows, no?'

'It does,' said the guide. 'But it is actually shaped like Lord Krishna's crown and all the windows are supposed to be the jewels in it.'

'What?' Kavya and Pia exclaimed together and ran towards the rows of windows on the third floor. They looked around and through the niches in the wall, but there was nothing!

'I think we are late again,' sighed Kavya.

'Hmmm...but look what I found, Didi,' Pia announced as she opened out her fist to show Kavya a tiny bead on her palm. 'It's from the charm hanging from the bag. I found it on the ledge of the third window – which means that the White Bishop came here, left the bag on the ledge of the window and someone else came and picked it up.'

'Well deduced, my tubelight!' said Kavya. 'But who would have taken the bag and where?'

'Maybe the next lines in the poem will make the picture clear,' said Pia. 'But look at the bead carefully, Didi. It has a small fort-like thing drawn on it.'

Kavya nodded. 'What do the next lines in the poem say?'

Pia took out the piece of paper from her pocket and read out: *'Ride to the beautiful hills of shadows and sound... There you will find a fireball, big and very round.'*

'Now where will we find these *beautiful hills of shadows and sound*?' Kavya's brow creased into a puzzled frown.

Their thoughts were suddenly broken by the clattering feet that rang out through the staircase. A group of tourists were climbing up the stairs. 'The Hawa Mahal is made of red and pink sandstone,' the guide accompanying the tourists was telling them. 'There's a fort on the outskirts of Jaipur which is also made of red and pink sandstone and marble. It's on the beautiful Aravalli hills. I will take you there tomorrow – the sound-and-light show that happens there is not to be missed.'

Kavya's mouth fell open. She stared at the group of tourists and the guide.

Pia snapped her fingers. 'The beautiful hills of shadows and sounds!' she exclaimed.

'Shhh!' said Kavya.

Kavya and Pia scampered down the staircase to where their parents were.

'Where is Guide Uncle?' asked Pia.

'He's gone out to take a phone call,' said Mamma.

A minute later, the guide came back.

'Guide Uncle, is there a big fort on the hills in Jaipur?' Pia asked with the excitement of a hunter hot on a scent.

'Yes, there is!' said the guide. 'There's the Amer Fort on the beautiful Aravalli hills. Before Jaipur, Amer was the capital of Rajasthan. But...I'm sorry, I won't be able to take you there. I have some important business to attend to.'

'We're not going to Amer Fort either,' Mamma declared. 'I have to do some jewellery shopping and we're going to Johri Bazaar after this.'

'B-O-R-I-N-G!' said Kavya, folding her arms.

'We want to go to Amer Fort!' said Pia, stomping her feet.

'While returning from Amer Fort, we can go to Johri Bazaar,' suggested Papa.

'Yes, yes. On our way back, we can go to the jewellery bazaar,' said Kavya and Pia.

'Promise?' asked Mamma.

'Pakka promise!' chorused Kavya and Pia.

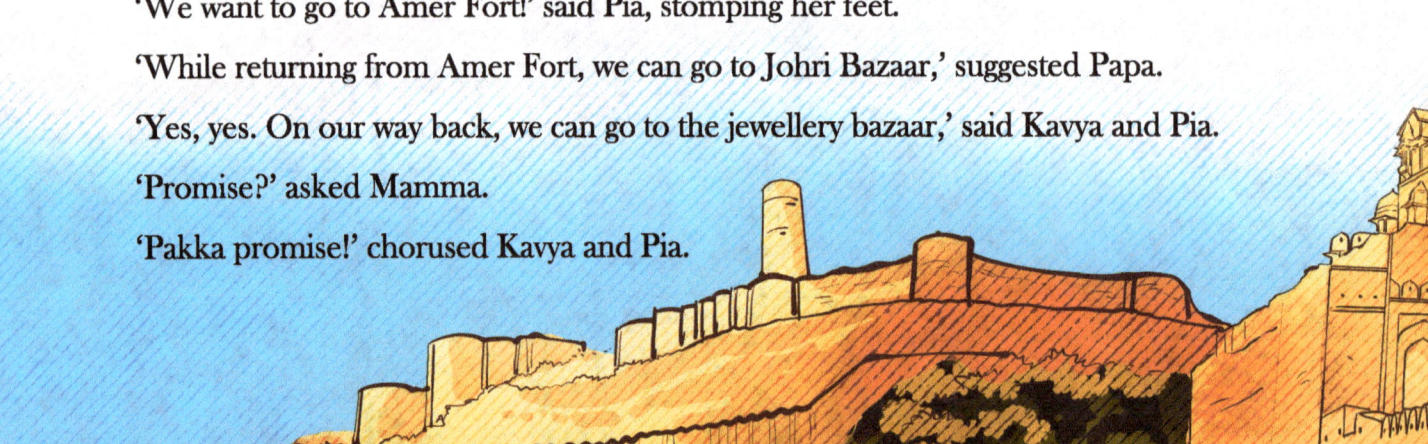

The family found themselves a taxi and left for Amer Fort. The taxi made its way through the rugged Aravalli hills and, in about twenty minutes, entered the ramparts of the fort. The entire setting was grand. This walled world of the Rajput rulers appeared to Kavya and Pia as something straight out of their history textbooks.

'This courtyard at the entrance is called the Jaleb Chowk,' the driver told them as the taxi came to a halt. 'It's here that the Maharaja's soldiers assembled and paraded themselves around.'

'You can head inside from here and take the staircase from the courtyard to reach the second courtyard that houses Diwan-e-Aam, Hall of Audience,' the driver added as Papa handed over the money to him.

'So this is where the Maharaja listened to the requests and complaints of the public,' said Mamma as they stood inside Diwan-e-Aam.

The carvings on the walls and ceilings of the Palace were intricate. Kavya and Pia looked at them, greatly astonished.

Then, through an ornate gate, the family made their way to where the Maharaja's private quarters were located. It had two buildings separated by a beautiful, geometrically designed garden. And the most exquisite of all was the palace of mirrors, the Sheesh Mahal.

'Look Didi, so many of me!' said Pia as she made faces looking at the mirrors in the walls of Sheesh Mahal.

But Kavya wasn't listening. She was lost in thoughts.

'Didi!' Pia nudged Kavya. 'What are you thinking?'

'About the sixth line in the poem,' said Kavya. 'We've reached the *beautiful hills of shadows and sounds* but where would we find *the fireball big and very round*?'

'It must be somewhere here, Didi,' said Pia. 'Let's look for it!'

As Papa and Mamma waited in the Sheesh Mahal, Pia and Kavya walked through the various pavilions and looked everywhere they could, but the mystery of the 'fireball' was not an easy one to solve.

'The fireball makes no sense,' Kavya sighed with disappointment as they walked back to the Sheesh Mahal.

Mamma and Papa were sitting on the stairs leading to the Sheesh Mahal.

'We met a group of tourists,' Papa told them. 'They were going to another fort which is connected to this fort through a secret passage that was created to provide an easy escape to the royal family in the times of war or siege. It's a ten-minute climb from here. Should we go and see that fort?' he asked.

'No, Papa,' said Kavya. 'We're tired. Let's go back.'

'We won't have to walk...we can take a golf cart,' said Mamma.

'Ummm...okay,' said Kavya.

On a golf cart, Kavya, Pia, Mamma and Papa reached a small hillock which, they were told, is Cheel ka Teela or the Hill of Eagles. It provided an excellent view of the Aravalli Hills.

The cart stopped in front of Jaigarh Fort, or the fort of victory. The information board at the entrance said that the fort was a defence structure built in 1726 by Maharaja Jai Singh and was never captured. It has survived intact through the centuries.

Inside the fort there were reservoirs, residential areas, whimsical-hatted lookout towers and even a puppet theatre. But the thing that caught everyone's eyes was a huge cannon.

As their parents were checking out the reservoir, Kavya and Pia walked towards the cannon.

'Is this real?' asked Pia, looking at the big cannon with her mouth agape.

'Look at this wooden plaque here,' said Kavya. 'This cannon is called the Jaivana cannon, the knell of victory. This fort was one the most efficient cannon foundries in the world.'

'That's right,' said a man in an ill-fitted khaki uniform, emerging from behind the wooden axle that ran under the cannon. He had a duster in his hand and seemed to be cleaning the cannon. 'The iron ore used for making the cannons in Jaigarh Fort came from the neighbouring villages which were rich in iron. A massive wind tunnel sucked air from the mountains into the furnace to create high temperature to melt the metal. The molten metal was then used to make big cannons. This cannon that you see is the biggest of all. Its barrel is 20.2 metres long and it weighs 50 tonnes. It can shoot a cannonball weighing 50 kilograms.'

'Has it ever fired a cannonball?' asked Pia, her eyes as big as saucers.

'Only once. It created a depression in a nearby village that eventually became a pond,' the man answered. 'Much work to finish, I have to go,' he said and left hurriedly.

Kavya walked around the cannon to examine it. 'It must be somewhere here,' she said.

'What, Didi?' asked Pia.

'The fireball, what else?'

And sure enough, on the other side was a stack of cannonballs. Pia reached over and tried to pick one of them up. It wouldn't budge.

Kavya shook her head. 'They're cemented down, silly girl!'

'You're right,' said Pia. 'Why do you suppose they've done that?'

'The village doesn't need another pond, I guess!' said Kavya. 'Look behind the platform on which the cannonballs are stacked!'

Pia's eyes flashed in excitement. 'There's something in here!' she said.

'What's it?' asked Kavya.

'TADA!' said Pia, in a manner of a conjurer pulling a rabbit out of his hat. 'The bag!'

Kavya and Pia opened the bag excitedly but there was nothing in it – it was empty as a skull.

'Where's the pouch?' asked Kavya, greatly flustered.

'The robbers are faster than us,' said Pia. 'Didi, did you look at the uniform of the man who was cleaning the cannon. It had a logo which looked similar to the fort drawn on the bead. Could he be the one?'

'Maybe,' said Kavya and dumped the bag behind the cannonballs.

'Now what, Didi?' asked Pia.

'What are the next lines in the poem?'

'Walk to the bazaar where trinkets are sold...Look for the shop with painted riches quite old.'

'There are so many bazaars in Jaipur. Which one the poem is talking about?'

Just then, Mamma came looking for them. 'Done?' she asked. 'Now let's go back to the city and do some jewellery shopping.'

'Do we have to, Mamma?' asked Kavya.

'You girls promised!' said Mamma, shrugging her shoulders.

Papa booked a taxi which arrived shortly after. As Pia was boarding the cab, she suddenly stopped in her tracks.

'What happened?' asked Kavya.

'I think I saw Guide Uncle,' said Pia.

'Where?' asked Kavya.

'In the taxi just ahead of us,' Pia answered.

'I don't see anybody,' said Kavya. 'And he'd said he has some work to finish. Why would he come here then?'

'Maybe I saw someone else,' said Pia.

As the taxi descended the hills, the evening lights of the city looked like small stars twinkling far away.

Soon, it reached the busy streets of the city, with shops of all kinds on both sides – some selling beautiful clothes with mirror work, some selling leather bags, some selling chappals and jootis, some selling colourful lac bangles and some selling pottery and marble products.

The cab went around a bend and stopped in front of a market that had small shops which looked identical in their size and colour. They were all painted orange, terracotta, and burnt pink.

SHOPPING ALERT

There are many bazaars in Jaipur, such as:

Bapu Bazaar, famous for its saris and fabrics

Sireh Deori Bazaar, famous for its jewellery shops

Kishanpol Bazaar, famous for textiles (especially bandhani)

Nehru Bazaar, famous for fabric and footwear (especially jootis)

Manihoron Rasta, famous for bangles

'Madam, want precious stones?' a man asked Mamma as she got down from the taxi. 'Emeralds, rubies, sapphires...'

'Do you have a shop here?' asked Mamma. 'We would like to buy some earrings.'

'Yes, Madam,' said the man. 'We have a shop at the end of this street. You will find all kinds of earrings with precious and semi-precious stones in our shop. This way, Madam...'

JEWELLERY IN JAIPUR

After founding Jaipur, Maharaja Jai Singh II is said to have organized a procession through the city where local crowds showered precious stones on him. He was very fond of jewels and, under his patronage, Jaipur started to become a centre of jewellery.

Amid the din of shoppers, the salesman led the family through the corridor which was lined with dozens of shops displaying magnificent necklaces, earrings, bracelets and rings. The salesman showed them to his shop which had glass cabinets on all walls. He then laid out several velvet-lined trays of earrings. There were earrings that had little peacocks studded with tiny gems, delicate filigreed butterflies in deep colours and many other beautiful designs.

But Kavya and Pia watched disinterestedly. Their minds were stuck on the poem.

Suddenly, Pia jerked up a little. 'I think I saw Guide Uncle passing through this shop!' she said.

'What's wrong with you, Pia?' asked Kavya. 'You're seeing Guide Uncle everywhere. Think about the next lines of the poem.'

'I am thinking about them, Didi. But let's go and check once. I'm sure it was Guide Uncle.'

'Uh-ho!' mumbled Kavya as Pia dragged her by her hand and came out of the shop.

In the twilight, they both saw a small, bald man walking a little ahead of them. 'He does look like the guide from behind,' said Kavya.

'Let's follow him, Didi!' pleaded Pia.

The man walked to a corner where three other people were waiting for him. The girls froze looking at these three people – they were the moustached man whom Pia had bumped into in the morning, the man with the unusually long neck whom they'd spotted at Jantar Mantar, and the man in the ill-fitted khaki uniform who was cleaning the cannon at Jaigarh Fort!

'We will have to be careful, Pia,' instructed Kavya. 'We don't want them to see us,' she added.

The sisters followed the guide and his friends to a shop that was on a slight elevation. The cabinets in the shop were decked with beautiful gilt-framed miniature paintings.

'Oh, so this is the shop with the painted riches,' murmured Kavya.

RAJPUT MINIATURES

The historic city of Jaipur was also one of the centres of Rajput miniature paintings. This style of painting flourished in the royal courts of Rajasthan in the seventeenth and eighteenth centuries by artists who were traditionally trained in the Mughal courts. They started illustrating the Hindu epics on sheets of paper and walls of palaces and havelis in natural colours which developed into the Rajput miniature style of painting.

Even today, Jaipur is home to some artists who practice this art form.

The guide and his friends climbed up the stairs. The sisters followed suit.

'Let's hide behind this pillar,' Kavya instructed Pia.

From behind the pillar, Kavya and Pia could hear a noisy scuffle.

'Arrey, what have you guys done?' the owner of the shop was shouting. 'The stones in this brooch aren't real!'

'H...h...how can that be, Hukum sa?' the guide stammered.

'I'm telling you,' said the owner. 'I just checked the stones.'

'Check again!' ordered the moustached man. 'How can a brooch straight out of the palace be fake?' he said angrily.

'Someone has fooled us!' the owner exclaimed, wiping away the beads of sweat on his forehead with the end of his long, colourful bandhani pugri. 'All these are just pieces of glass, not jewels!'

Just then, Mamma and Papa came looking for Kavya and Pia, with a policeman in tow. 'We have been looking for you for so long! Why did you come here without telling us? Luckily we found the Police Inspector in the market and...'

'Shhh...! We've found out who stole the Maharaja's brooch!' whispered an excited Kavya and pointed inside. The sisters told the inspector and their parents about the poem and how they had been trying to solve the mystery.

The Inspector peered inside and let out a gasp. 'At last!' he murmured to himself.

'Freeze! Hands up!' said the policeman in a stern voice as he entered the shop.

'Bhaaaaago!!!' screamed the shop-owner and made a run towards the door, followed by the other members of his gang.

The Inspector raced across and blocked the entrance.

Soon, other policemen too appeared on the scene. The Inspector had made a quick call at the Police Station to send a part of their force.

'Now spend your time in the prison working out the mystery of the fake brooch – how about writing a poem about that?' the Inspector looked at the shop-owner scornfully and said. 'Do you think the royal family is so naïve to keep the real brooch on display?' he added.

'You girls are absolutely remarkable!' said the Inspector turning to Kavya and Pia. 'You helped us nab this notorious gang!'

Kavya and Pia smiled broadly.

The Inspector shoved the gang of robbers into his jeep and drove away.

'See! Didn't I say that palaces are always full of mystery,' said Pia.

'Right, my little detective!' said Mamma.

'Papa, can we come to Jaipur next year as well?' asked Kavya, with a note of triumph in her voice.

'And the year after that?' added Pia.

'Done!' said Papa with a laugh. 'How about going back to the hotel and having something to eat for now?' he asked.

10 things to eat

1. Dal Baati Choorma
2. Pyaaz ki Kachori
3. Aloo Tikkis
4. Lassi
5. Rabri-ghevar
6. Kulfi-falooda
7. Chooran
8. Chilla
9. Jalebi
10. Mirchi Pakoras

10 things to do

1. Listen to the folk musicians at Chowki Dhani
2. Witness the vast flora and fauna at Nahargarh Biological Park
3. Stroll around the rose garden at Jawahar Circle
4. Go for a picnic at Ramgarh Lake
5. Visit Jawahar Kala Kendra
6. Enjoy the breathtaking view of the city of Jaipur from the Ishwar Lat minaret near the City Palace
7. Go boating on the Man Sagar Lake and soak in the beauty of the magnificent Jal Mahal
8. Shop for blue pottery at Jaipur Blue Pottery Art Centre
9. Revel in an adventure at Jhalana Leopard Safari
10. See one of the six Egyptian mummies at Albert Hall Museum

10 things to see

1. Jaipur Wax Museum
2. Anokhi Museum of Hand Printing
3. Panna Meena ki Baoli
4. Masala Chowk
5. Sisodia Rani Garden
6. Galtaji
7. Birla Temple
8. Gatore ki Chattriyan
9. Jal Mahal
10. Diggi Palace

GLOSSARY

Bandhani: a type of tie-and-dye textile

Bhaago: run

Chappals: slippers

Chowk: an intersection or roundabout

Gangajalis: urns with the water from the Ganges

Jooti: a type of footwear with extensive embroidery

Khamma Ghani: hello or welcome

Mirchi Pakodas: fritters made from hot green chilies

Paani ke Bataashe: hollow fried balls stuffed with potatoes and filled with flavoured water

Padharo Sa: please come

Pyaaz Kachori: a fried pastry filled with a spicy onion filling

Tuk-tuk: a local three-wheeled autorickshaw

THE GOLDEN TOURISM TRIANGLE

Jaipur is a part of the Golden Tourism Triangle of the country. The other two cities that form this triangle are Delhi and Agra. It means that Jaipur is one amongst the most visited places in India.

About Indian National Trust for Art and Cultural Heritage (INTACH)

INTACH is a nationwide, non-profit membership organization to protect and conserve India's vast natural and cultural heritage. It is today the largest organization in the country dedicated to conservation. Heritage Education and Communication Service (HECS) of INTACH spreads awareness about India's natural, built, cultural, and living heritage. HECS promotes a love for heritage amongst children. It runs a network of heritage clubs. Each heritage club works on promoting the local culture and appreciating the rich diversity of India's heritage.

For further details, log on to: www. intach.org, www.youngintach.org

About Talking Cub

Talking Cub is the children's imprint of Speaking Tiger Books. Launched in December 2017, the imprint has published over fifty books, including those by renowned authors such as Ruskin Bond, Paro Anand, Ranjit Lal, Subhadra Sen Gupta, Deepa Agarwal and others. Some of the country's best fiction and non-fiction writing for children is part of the imprint. The details of all the titles can be seen at www.speakingtigerbooks.com.

Arthy Muthanna Singh is a children's writer, freelance journalist, copywriter, editor and cartoonist. She has a diverse range of experience in the publishing industry, a large part of it spent at *Limca Book of Records*. She has authored many books for children. She conducts creative writing workshops and dreams of moving to Goa some day.

Mamta Nainy is a children's writer based in New Delhi. She spent some years in advertising before an apple fell on her head while she was sitting under a mango tree, and she had her Eureka moment. She has been writing for children since then. She loves travelling but when she's too lazy to do it, she makes do with reading. She can usually be spotted next to a pile of children's books, chuckling to herself!

Priyankar Gupta is a pre-visualizer and a creative consultant in the field of media, advertising and broadcast design. He has worked with various publishing companies across the globe as an illustrator for children's book and books for young adults. He has been a mentor in various design schools across the country, teaching various forms of visual narratives.